QUICK INTRO GUIDE
TO COMPUTER SCIENCE 2
WITH C++

A BRIEF INTRODUCTION TO DATA STRUCTURES AND ALGORITHMS

BY JOHN P. BAUGH

Published: May, 2013
ISBN-13:   978-1489586094
ISBN-10:   1489586091

TABLE OF CONTENTS

CONTENTS

Who's This Book For? 7

About the Author 7

What you need 8

Resources, Making Suggestions and Errors 9

Chapter 1: Review of Classes 10

1.1   Introduction to Classes and OOP 10

1.2   Creating a project and files in Visual Studio 11

1.2.1   Creating the project 11

1.2.2   Adding Source code to the Project 12

1.2.2   Creating files for our class 15

Chapter 2: Unordered Linked Lists 22

2.1   Introduction to Unordered Linked Lists 22

2.2   Conceptual Overview 23

2.2.1   The Node Class 24

2.2.2   The UnorderedList Class 25

2.3   UnorderedList Implementation 27

2.3.1   UnorderedList Specification File (.H) 27

2.3.2   UnorderedList Skeleton Implementation File (.cPP) 28

2.3.3   Member Function Implementations 29

2.3.3.1   The Constructor and Destructor 30

2.3.3.2   IsFull and IsEmpty 30

2.3.3.3   GetItem... 32

2.3.3.4   MakeEmpty 33

2.3.3.5   Insert... 34

2.3.3.6   RemoveItem... 34

2.3.3.7   PrintList 37

2.4   Full Source Listing 37

2.4.1   UnorderedList.h.. 37

2.4.2   UnorderedList.cpp 38

2.4.3   Main.cpp – a sample driver program 41

Chapter 3: Ordered Linked Lists 43

3.1   Introduction to Ordered Linked Lists.. 43

3.2   Conceptual Overview 43

3.2.1   The Node Class 44

3.2.2   The OrderedList Class 44

3.3   OrderedList Implementation... 46

3.3.1   OrderedList Specification File (.H)... 47

3.3.2   OrderedList Member Function Implementations 47

3.3.2.1   Insert.. 48

3.4   Full Source Listing 51

3.4.1   OrderedList.h.. 51

3.4.2   OrderedList.cpp 52

3.4.3   Main.cpp – A Sample Driver program 54

Chapter 4: Stacks 57

4.1   Introduction to Stacks 57

4.2   Conceptual Overview.. 57

4.2.1   The Node Class 58

4.2.2   The Stack ClasS 58

4.3   Stack Implementation... 60

4.3.1   Stack Specification File (.H) 60

4.3.2   Stack Member Function Implementations 61

4.3.2.1   Constructor and Destructor.. 61

4.3.2.2   IsFull and IsEmpty 61

4.3.2.3   Push 62

4.3.2.4   Pop.. 63

4.3.2.5   Top... 64

4.3.2.6   MakeEmpty... 64

4.3.2.7   PrintStack 65

4.4   Full Source Listing 65

4.4.1   Stack.h.. 65

4.4.2   Stack.cpp 66

4.4.3   Main.cpp – A Sample Driver Program 68

Chapter 5: Queues 70

5.1   Introduction to Queues 70

5.2   Conceptual Overview 70

5.2.1   The Node Class 70

5.2.2   The Queue Class 71

5.3   Queue Implementation 73

5.3.1   Queue Specification File (.H) 73

5.3.2   Queue Member Function Implementations 74

5.3.2.1   Constructor and Destructor 74

5.3.2.2   IsFull and isEmpty 74

5.3.2.3   Enqueue 75

5.3.2.4   Dequeue 77

5.3.2.5   MakeEmpty 79

5.3.2.6   PrintQueue 79

5.4   Full Source Listing 80

5.4.1   Queue.h 80

5.4.2   Queue.cpp 80

5.4.3   Main.cpp – A Sample Driver Program 83

Chapter 6: Sorting 85

6.1   Introduction to Sorting 85

6.1.2   A very brief introduction to complexity analysis 85

6.1.3   A Handy Print Function 86

6.2   Bubble Sort – A Classic Example of Exchange Sorts 86

6.2.1   An Implementation of BubbleSort 87

6.2.2   AN Entire Source File Using BubbleSort 88

6.2.3   A Closer Look at the above sorting process 90

6.3   Selection Sort 91

6.3.1   An Implementation of Selection Sort 92

6.3.2   An Entire Source File using Selection Sort 93

6.3.3   A Closer Look at the above sorting process 95

6.4   Insertion Sort 96

6.4.1   An Implementation of Insertion Sort 96

6.4.2   An Entire Source File Using Insertion Sort 97

6.4.3   A Closer Look at the Above Sorting Process 98

Appendix A 100

A-1   Exception Handling 100

A-1.1   Revisiting our Stack Class with Exception Handling 100

Index Of Terms 105

WHO'S THIS BOOK FOR?

This book is for anyone who has at least a semester of C++ programming knowledge and who wants to understand several intermediate C++ topics. Although I try to be thorough and clear, I also take a less intimidating and less formal approach to teaching, and a lot of people learn better that way – maybe you're one of them!

If you are familiar with the following topics (not necessarily an expert, but familiar and relatively comfortable with most of them), then you should be fine:

- declaring and using variables
- strings
- basic user input and output using the `iostream` library, and `cin` and `cout` variables
- file I/O using `ifstream` and `ofstream` data types found in the `fstream` library
- selection control structures (`if`, `if-else`, `switch`)
- repetition control structures (`while`, `do-while`, `for`)
- arrays
- pointers
- basic exception handling
- ability to create `class`es and `struct`s

This book will cover some of the commonly studied topics in Computer Science 2 (Intermediate Computer Science) courses across the world. It is by no means an exhaustive textbook on all possible intermediate topics within C++. This book is for the purpose of introducing you several common topics discussed in such a course, or as a review of such topics. This makes an excellent (and much cheaper!) companion guide to your class textbook. It's also suitable for self-teachers.

ABOUT THE AUTHOR

My name is John P. Baugh, and I'm a full-time Professor of Computer Science at Oakland Community College – Orchard Ridge in Farmington Hills, Michigan. I'm also an adjunct lecturer for the Department of Computer Science at the University of Michigan – Dearborn in Dearborn, Michigan, as well as Schoolcraft College in Livonia, Michigan.

I hold a Master of Science degree in Computer Science from the University of Michigan – Dearborn, and I am currently working on a Ph.D. in Information Systems Engineering.

I worked as a researcher in the Vehicular Networking Systems Research Laboratory (VNSRL) under Dr. Jinhua Guo from 2005 until I completed my Masters in 2007. I was then hired as a software engineer for Siemens PLM Software in Ann Arbor, Michigan where I worked until I was appointed as a professor at OCC. I've taught in one form or another since 2003 courses including Computer Science I, Computer Science II (both with C++, university undergraduate level), Discrete Mathematics, Visual Basic, Java, Object-Oriented Programming with C++, Advanced Networking (Graduate/Masters Degree level), Microsoft Office, System Support, C#, Game Development, and several other courses.

I love teaching, playing my violin, writing software for side projects that I have, playing video games on my Xbox 360 and on the PC (and even occasionally on my mobile phone), and hanging with my crazy friends from church. Oh, and not to forget – last but certainly not least – writing educational materials dealing mostly with programming and other tech-related topics.

WHAT YOU NEED

You basically just need a computer and a compiler/IDE that you can compile and debug C++ code with. I will be using Visual Studio Professional 2012, which you may be able to get for free from your university or college (through Dreamspark.com) or you can download the VS 2012 Express Edition and that should work just fine. C++ is platform-independent for the code that we'll be using so even if you're using another IDE like Code::Blocks or Dev-C++ or even an IDE on another platform like XCode on MacOS X, you should be just fine.

Since this is an intermediate book, I do assume you have familiarity with an IDE by now, and the topics described earlier.

RESOURCES, MAKING SUGGESTIONS AND ERRORS

For more information, errata (that's academic talk for boo-boos I make in the book), and other resources, check my website out at:

www.profjpbaugh.com

I hope to provide clarifications, more information on my blogs and information about my upcoming books and software I'm working on.

Also – if you have specific suggestions or think certain points in the book need clarification, or would love to see a particular topic or application of specific data structures or algorithms, ***just e-mail me*** at ***profjpbaugh@gmail.com***. I will try to find the time to post more tutorials based on feedback on the book. I try to be as active as I can with my tutorial set and blogs on computer-related topics. Contacting me and voicing what you want to see will be far more beneficial for us both than complaining on a review message board or forum. ☺

CHAPTER 1:
REVIEW OF CLASSES

1.1   INTRODUCTION TO CLASSES AND OOP

In this section, we'll do a brief review of how to create a **class** and how to instantiate **objects**.

Conceptually, you might need a quick review of terminology, so think of a *class* as a blueprint, and an *object* as the thing created from the blueprint. For example, let's say you have a blueprint for a car. The blueprint contains information about the number of doors, the type of engine, the color of the car, etc. However, you can't *drive* the blueprint. You need a car to be made from the blueprint.

In terms of **object-oriented programming** (**OOP**), you design a class (blueprint) and then you **instantiate**, or create instances (objects) of the class. The objects, or instances, therefore, would be like the actual car being made from the blueprint.

Often, C++ programmers create two separate files to make a class, the **specification file**, which usually ends in .h (also called a header file) that contains the **public** and **private** (and sometimes **protected**) **data members** and **member functions** of the class, but doesn't contain any implementation – just the prototypes/function headers. The second file, the **implementation file**, usually ends in .cpp and includes the specification file and contains the actual *how* behind the *what* of the class. In other words, the implementation file contains the... implementation! Fancy that, huh?

1.2   CREATING A PROJECT AND FILES IN VISUAL STUDIO

Here are the steps to create a new project in Visual Studio Professional 2012. Note that a **solution** is a collection of one or more **projects**, and a **project** is a collection of source files and other resources.

1.2.1   CREATING THE PROJECT

1. Open up Visual Studio 2012
2. Go to File→New→Project

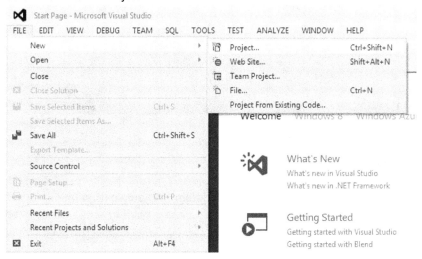

3. Make sure you are under Visual C++ as the language, and that you have Win32 Console Application selected as the project type.
4. Give the solution a meaningful name (such as Ch1_FirstProg or Ch1_ReviewClasses or something else meaningful), and if you wish, change the directory that the solution will be in

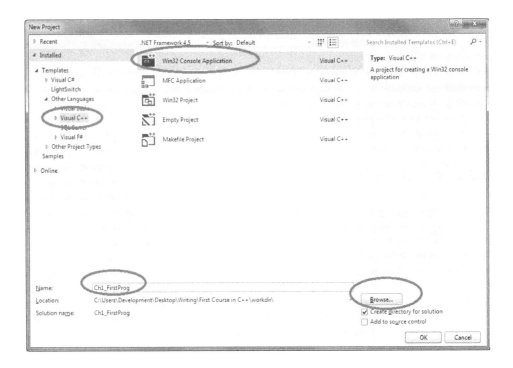

5. Press OK
6. Go under Application Settings to the left
7. Verify that Console Application is selected from the Radio button Menu
8. Check the Empty Project Box
9. Press Finish

Note that this will automatically create a solution to contain the project.

1.2.2 ADDING SOURCE CODE TO THE PROJECT

Here's how you add a new source file to your project:

1. Under Solution Explorer, right-click the folder named **Source Files**
2. Go to Add→New Item

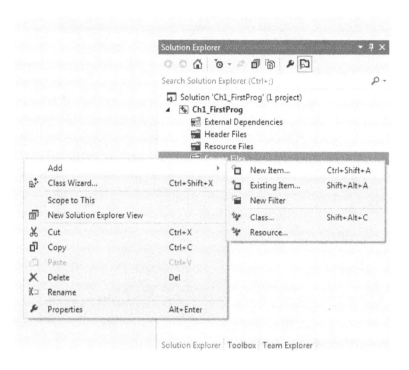

3. Select C++ File (.cpp) (or if a header, use .h)
4. Give the file a meaningful name – I named mine ***main.cpp***
5. Hit Add

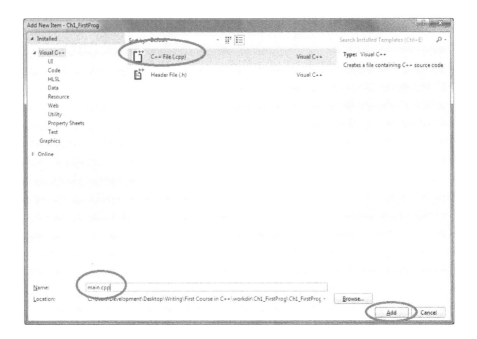

And that's it! You now have a new source file added to your project.

1.2.2 CREATING FILES FOR OUR CLASS

We're going to create a class to represent a car.

Using the steps described above to ensure you have all three files described below.

File	Type	Description
main.cpp	C++ File (.cpp)	This file will act as the "driver" file. You will use this to house the main function, and you will create instances (objects) of the Car class. **Add this to the Source Files section in the Solution Explorer.**
Car.h	Header File (.h)	This is the *specification file*. It will contain the basic description of the Car class, and the private data members. **Make sure to add this file to the section marked "Header Files" in the Solution Explorer**
Car.cpp	C++ File (.cpp)	This is the *implementation file*. It will contain the actual implementation. **Add this to the Source Files section in the Solution Explorer.**

The result should be three empty files in your project:

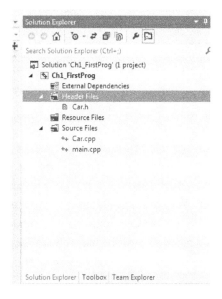

15

```
1   #include <iostream>
2   #include "Car.h"
3   using namespace std;
4
5   int main()
6   {
7
8           return 0;
9   }
```

main.cpp

This file is self explanatory, yet incomplete. We will add more to it later.

The next element we want to define is the class itself. We want the following private data:

Data Member	Data Type	Purpose
year	int	Represents the year the car was manufactured in
make	string	The company that made the vehicle
model	string	The model of the vehicle

For each of the above, we want to have two different types of member functions"

Getters (also known as **accessors**) *get* data from the class but do not modify the contents of the class. It is good practice, but not required, to use the word **const** after the header of the member function. This will ensure that *if* you accidentally try to modify data in the class, you will get a compiler error. The `const` keyword is used frequently to mean different things in C++ (for example, a `const` variable is simply a variable that cannot be modified once it is instantiated.) But, when `const` comes after a member function name, it is basically like signing a contract with the class saying, "This member function won't mess with your internal data – it's just for peeking inside the class." You can think of it as declaring a member function to treat data members as *read-only*.

Setters (also known as **mutators**) *set* data in the class. They can modify the class's internal data and thus, do not sign the "`const` contract" with the class like setters do.

Here are the member functions that we want:

Function Name	Notes / Access Type	Description
getYear	Getter	Returns the `year` (an int)
getMake	Getter	Returns the `make` of the vehicle (a string)
getModel	Getter	Returns the `model` of the vehicle (a string)
setYear	Setter	Sets the internal `year` data member
setMake	Setter	Sets the internal `make` data member
setModel	Setter	Sets the internal `model` data member
Car( )	Constructor	Sets the default values for `year`, `make`, and `model`

Okay, so now let's set up the specification (.h) file. Remember that we don't typically define the entire class in this file, just the private data members, and the *what* of the class, not the *how*. In other words, no implementation.

```
1    #ifndef CAR_H
2    #define CAR_H
3
4    #include <string>
5    using namespace std;
6
7    class Car
8    {
9    public:
10          Car();
11          void setYear(int y);
12          void setMake(string m);
13          void setModel(string m);
14
15          int getYear() const;
16          string getMake() const;
17          string getModel() const;
18
19   private:
20          int year;
21          string make;
22          string model;
23   };
24
25   #endif
```

Car.h – the specification file for our Car class

One thing you might notice right away is that on lines 1 and 2, and line 25, there are preprocessor directives called **macros**. What we're doing here is, on line 1, testing if a macro variable named CAR_H exists. If it *is not defined*, we move to line 2 and then the rest of the class. If it is defined, we skip down to line 25. We define the macro variable CAR_H on line 2, so this means that if we include this file in multiple locations, we will only have one definition for our class that ever occurs. This can be a big problem on some platforms and with some compilers, and it's just considered good coding practice, although not necessarily required.

Also note that we put the `const` keyword after all the getter member functions on lines 15-17. And of course, don't forget in C++, you must put a semicolon after the closing curly brace, as it is on line 23.

Now, let's see the implementation file.

```
1    #include "Car.h"
2
3    Car::Car()
4    {
5            year = 0;
6            make = "";
7            model = "";
8    }
9
10   void Car::setYear(int y)
11   {
12           year = y;
13   }
14
15   void Car::setMake(string m)
16   {
17           make = m;
18   }
19
20   void Car::setModel(string m)
21   {
22           model = m;
23   }
24
25   int Car::getYear() const
26   {
27           return year;
28   }
29
30   string Car::getMake() const
31   {
32           return make;
33   }
34
35   string Car::getModel() const
36   {
37           return model;
38   }
```

Car.cpp – the implementation file

This file includes the Car.h file, and simply implements the member functions. Recall from your previous excursions into C++, that you must put the name of the class and the **scope resolution operator**, : :, in front of the names of the member functions. Other than that, this is a very straightforward implementation.

Finally, we make use of the class by creating a couple objects of the type Car, and using their member functions.

```
1    #include <iostream>
2    #include "Car.h"
3    using namespace std;
4
5    int main()
6    {
7           Car myCar;
8           Car yourCar;
9
10          myCar.setYear(2007);
11          myCar.setMake("Ford");
12          myCar.setModel("Focus");
13
14          yourCar.setYear(1970);
15          yourCar.setMake("Plymouth");
16          yourCar.setModel("Barracuda");
17
18          cout<<"My car is a "<<myCar.getYear()<<" ";
19          cout<<myCar.getMake()<<" "<<myCar.getModel()<<endl;
20
21          cout<<"Your car is a "<<yourCar.getYear()<<" ";
22          cout<<yourCar.getMake()<<" "<<yourCar.getModel()<<endl;
23
24          return 0;
25   }
```

main.cpp – the driver file

We include the specification file on line 2, and then on lines 7 and 8, create two objects of the type Car. We then call the methods to set the data on lines 10-16 for the two Car objects.

Finally, on lines 18-22, we print out the data that is stored in the objects.

This is a pretty straightforward implementation.

Note that if we wanted to, we could also declare pointers to the Car variables, and create the objects on the **heap** (free store) using the new keyword, as in the following example.

```
1    #include <iostream>
2    #include "Car.h"
3    using namespace std;
4
5    int main()
6    {
7            Car* myCar = new Car();
8            Car* yourCar = new Car();
9
10           myCar->setYear(2007);
11           myCar->setMake("Ford");
12           myCar->setModel("Focus");
13
14           yourCar->setYear(1970);
15           yourCar->setMake("Plymouth");
16           yourCar->setModel("Barracuda");
17
18           cout<<"My car is a "<<myCar->getYear()<<" ";
19           cout<<myCar->getMake()<<" "<<myCar->getModel()<<endl;
20
21           cout<<"Your car is a "<<yourCar->getYear()<<" ";
22           cout<<yourCar->getMake()<<" "<<yourCar->getModel()<<endl;
23
24           return 0;
25   }
```

main.cpp – driver file, this time using pointers and the arrow operator

Notice the difference in syntax. Often, it is a better choice to work with pointers to objects instead of working with the objects directly, for many reasons, but two of the following are major ones:

- Passing pointers to functions is must less computationally expensive than passing an entire object, especially in the cases of large objects
- If you have to dynamically create objects at run time and don't know how many you will need ahead of time, pointers are perfect for this task (as we shall see later in the book

CHAPTER 2:
UNORDERED LINKED LISTS

2.1   INTRODUCTION TO UNORDERED LINKED LISTS

In this chapter, we will begin our look into some of the stuff that confuses computer science students (and practitioners alike!) Namely, I'm talking about **linked structures**. Remember that I said a class provides *encapsulation*, which means partly that it hides the implementation from the individual using it, so they don't have to worry about the details – they just get to use the class.

Well, think about making a list of items as a class. Let's say you wanted to provide some functionality for adding, removing, and obtaining different items in the list. Regardless of *how you implement the class*, the user of the class will want the same functionality – they may want to call some sort of `Insert` member function, some sort of `Remove` member function, and so on.

How would you actually store the data "behind the scenes"? You have many options, but if we want our **unordered list** to grow automatically, we could use one of the following:

- A **dynamic array**
    - Every time we'd get to the bounds of our internal array, we would dynamically create an array with the `new` keyword and copy over the elements from the "old" array, and then delete that old array
- A **linked structure**
    - In this case, think of creating a new "node" every time we want to add an item, and then we hook the node into our list after it's created

Many books provide multiple implementations for the Unordered List **ADT (abstract data type)**, but by far it seems most students have trouble with the linked structure implementation, known as an **unordered linked list**, or an **unsorted linked list**.

2.2   CONCEPTUAL OVERVIEW

To implement a linked list, we need to create two classes:

- The Node class
    - This represents an individual item in the list
    - Has a data part, containing the data that is to be stored in the node
    - Has a pointer to the next item in the list, so it can be joined into the list
    - Since it is so simple, many programmers just implement the Node as a struct instead of a class
- The UnorderedList class
    - This represents a collection of Nodes, linked together
    - Contains a special pointer to the beginning of the list, called the **head** of the list

This can be visually described by the following diagram of a list with two nodes.

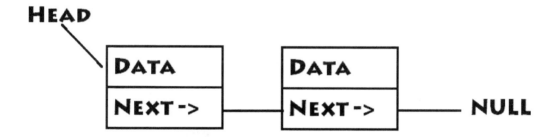

Notice that the head pointer variable of the list points to the first node in the list. Then, that node's next data member points to the *next* node in the list, and then that second node points to nullptr (or NULL if you're using a pre-C++ 11 compiler) with its next data member.

So, in a linked list of any size, the first node is pointed to by the head, and the last node's next points to nullptr. This is how we designate the beginning and end of lists.

So let's provide some more formal description of what kind of data and behavior we have to keep track of in our unordered list ADT.

2.2.1   THE NODE CLASS

First this unordered linked list, we're going to make it a list that keeps track of integers. This can be made general by using templates, but for clarity's sake, we'll use a specific data type for this example.

Data Member Name	Data Type	Description
mData	`int`	This data member of the Node class will hold the actual data that the list is trying to maintain. Each node holds a single integer.
mNext	`Node*`	This data member of the Node class is a *pointer* to another Node object. Specifically, in terms of how we are going to use it, it will point to the very next item in the linked list.

For this particular class, we're going to do something a little sneaky – perhaps frowned upon by some of the snobbier members of the programming community – but a legitimate technique. We're not going to have any member functions for this class.

How do we get the data out then? We're simply going to make the data in this class public so that it can be accessed directly. Since this class is only used in the `UnorderedList` class – these nodes are not intended to live outside of the context of our list's class – we make the data public. This is a technique used in software engineering called **composition**. The Node objects are intended to live inside the linked list, and the linked list is *composed* of Nodes.

2.2.2   THE UNORDEREDLIST CLASS

This class is going to be a full-fledged, encapsulated class. We have to determine what data we're going to maintain as private data members of the class, and what member functions we want to operate on the class.

First, the data member

Data Member Name	Data Type	Description
mHead	Node*	This data member points to the head of the list. When there are no Nodes in the list, mHead points to nullptr. Since each node points to the next node in the list, the list will be relatively self-structuring as we define the member functions

Now, the member functions

Member Function Name	Return type	Parameters	Description
UnorderedList	None (constructor)	None	This will initialize the list by setting the mHead variable to nullptr. Thus, the list starts empty.
~UnorderedList	None (destructor)	None	This will indirectly make the list empty again, removing all elements that are currently in the list, one at a time.
IsFull	bool	None	This returns if the list is full or not. In the case of a list that keeps creating nodes on the heap, you

			might think it would never be full. But this isn't the case. If there is no memory left, then the list is full. More on how we test if there's no memory left later.
IsEmpty	bool	None	This returns if the list is empty. In other words, does the `mHead` variable point to `nullptr?`
GetItem	Node*	`int item`	Returns a pointer to an object in the list if the `item` is found. Returns `nullptr` otherwise.
MakeEmpty	void	None	Makes the list empty. Removes all elements from the list.
InsertItem	void	`int item`	Inserts the item specified as a parameter as the first element in the list. Moves the former first element (head) of the list down.
RemoveItem	void	`int item`	Removes the item specified as a parameter if it exists.
PrintList	void	None	Prints the contents of the list

Okay, so we have something to work with, so let's write some actual code to get started. We may not know how to implement everything yet, but we at least have an idea of the types of functionality we want to support, and the data we need to maintain.

2.3   UNORDEREDLIST IMPLEMENTATION

Now that we have an idea of the design of the class itself, let's make some files.

File	Type	Description
main.cpp	C++ File (.cpp)	This is the *driver* file that we will use to test our class out.
UnorderedList.h	Header File (.h)	This is the specification file of our UnorderedList. We will also define the Node type in here.
UnorderedList.cpp	C++ File (.cpp)	This is the implementation file of our UnorderedList. We will implement the actual functions in here.

Start a new project, and add the three aforementioned files.

2.3.1   UNORDEREDLIST SPECIFICATION FILE (.H)

The file UnorderedList.h will contain the function prototypes for the members of the UnorderedList class as well as its data members. It will also contain the Node class definition, with its data members.

Recall that the members of the Node class are to be public. It has no private data, and no member functions whatsoever.

```
1    class Node
2    {
3    public:
4            int mData;
5            Node* mNext;
6    };
7
8    class UnorderedList
9    {
10   public:
11           UnorderedList();
12           ~UnorderedList();
13           bool IsFull() const;
14           bool IsEmpty() const;
15           Node* GetItem(int item);
16           void MakeEmpty();
17           void InsertItem(int item);
18           void RemoveItem(int item);
19           void PrintList();
20   private:
21           Node* mHead;
22
23   };
```

CUnorderedList.h – Specification file

For the most part, this is basically just putting our description from earlier in code form. The specification part is the easy part. The *implementation* part is the part that takes some thinking.

2.3.2   UNORDEREDLIST SKELETON IMPLEMENTATION FILE (.CPP)

We will treat each of the member functions separately, and then look at the entire implementation. But first, just get a "skeleton" of the implementations ready in the UnorderedList.cpp file.

```
1    #include "UnorderedList.h"
2    #include <new>
3    #include <iostream>
4
5    using namespace std;
6
7    UnorderedList::UnorderedList()
```

```
8    {
9
10   }
11
12   UnorderedList::~UnorderedList()
13   {
14
15   }
16
17   bool UnorderedList::IsFull() const
18   {
19
20   }
21
22   bool UnorderedList::IsEmpty() const
23   {
24
25   }
26
27   Node* UnorderedList::GetItem(int item)
28   {
29
30   }
31
32   void UnorderedList::MakeEmpty()
33   {
34
35   }
36   void UnorderedList::InsertItem(int item)
37   {
38
39   }
40
     void UnorderedList::RemoveItem(int item)
     {

     }
```

UnorderedList.cpp – the Implementation File skeleton – before we actually implement anything.

2.3.3   MEMBER FUNCTION IMPLEMENTATIONS

We will slowly build up our class by implementing our member functions in small "chunks", rather than seeing the whole implementation right off the bat. I want you to be able to think through *why* the different member functions are implemented the way they are.

2.3.3.1 THE CONSTRUCTOR AND DESTRUCTOR

The constructor will basically just set the `mHead` to `nullptr` and the destructor, since it is responsible for cleaning up (deleting) the entire list, will just call `MakeEmpty`. Since this is exactly what `MakeEmpty`'s job is, why should we write the same code twice?

```
1  UnorderedList::UnorderedList()
2  {
3        mHead = nullptr;
4  }
5
6  UnorderedList::~UnorderedList()
7  {
8        MakeEmpty();
9  }
```

And that's it for the constructor and destructor. These are pretty simple, right?

2.3.3.2 ISFULL AND ISEMPTY

In this subsection, we'll take a look at the `IsFull` and `IsEmpty` member functions. Conceptually, IsEmpty is *extremely* easy, and so is the IsFull function.

For `IsEmpty`, all we have to do is return whether or not the `mHead` variable is pointing to `nullptr` or not. If it is, then we know the list is empty. If it's not, then the list is *not* empty.

For `IsFull`, our task is a *little* more complicated, but only because you may not be familiar with performing a test to see if your system is simply out of memory.

Let's do the easy one first.

```
1  bool UnorderedList::IsEmpty() const
2  {
3        return mHead == nullptr;  //NULL if pre-C++ 11
4  }
```

We could use an if-statement if we wanted to, but think of how sleek the above code is. Since the member function IsEmpty returns a bool, we can just use a relational operator, in this case, the equality operator (==), which will evaluate to a Boolean value. Thus, we can use the simple one line of code that we have on line 3. Easy, breezy, and quick to write.

The harder of these two member functions is definitely IsFull. But it's really not that bad. You just need to know the basics of **exception handling** using try-catch statements – which I cover briefly in Appendix A. Recall that the block of code following a try keyword is the potentially "dangerous" code that could throw an exception. Recall that an **exception** is an error that occurs when something goes wrong in code at runtime.

The catch block is the code that we execute *if* an exception occurs. So basically, we define a list as being full if we simply don't have any more memory available to us to create another node. So cleverly, we will try to create a Node on the heap, and if there is no memory, we will receive a bad_alloc (bad allocation) exception. This exception's data type definition is made available to us in the new library, which is why we included it at the top of the file with the statement #include <new>.

So, here's the code.

```
1  bool UnorderedList::IsFull() const
2  {
3       try
4       {
5            Node* temp;
6            temp = new Node();
7            delete temp;
8            return false;
9       }
10      catch(bad_alloc ex)
11      {
12           return true;
13      }
14  }
```

In the try block, we simply attempt to create a node on the heap. If it fails, we immediately go to the return true in the catch block. If it succeeds, we immediately, delete the memory we just reserved. The delete keyword simply returns the memory occupied by temp back to the operating system. If we get to line 8 in the code, that means there were no problems, so the allocation succeeded, thus, we still have memory and return false.

2.3.3.3   GETITEM

If we want to retrieve a reference to a node in the list, we simply look through the list for the node whose data matches the item, and then return a reference to it.

```
1    Node* UnorderedList::GetItem(int item)
2    {
3         Node* temp = mHead;
4
5         while(temp!= nullptr)  //NULL if pre-C++ 11
6         {
7              if(temp->mData = item)
8              {
9                   return temp;
10             }
11             temp = temp->mNext;  //go to the next one
12        }
13
14        return nullptr;  //if never found, nust return NULL or nullptr
15   }
```

In this code on line 3, we create a variable, of type Node pointer (Node*) named temp and set it to point to the mHead. Note that this doesn't copy that node. Remember that a *pointer* contains a memory address.

You might ask why we don't just use mHead to move through the list. The reason we need a temporary variable for this task is because you must remember that mHead is a variable that needs to *always* point to the head of the list itself. If we start making statements like mHead = mHead->mNext, then we will lose track of the previous nodes in the list. Since we do not want to modify the structure of our linked list, just move through it, we use a temporary variable to do the walking through the list without losing the head of the list.

On lines 5-12, we look through the list until we find a node whose data matches the item parameter passed into the function. Moving forward in the list is what the code on line 11 is for. It causes the temporary pointer variable to point to the mNext of the current temp pointer. If the temp eventually equals nullptr, that means that we've gone through the whole list and have not found the item in question. So, the loop terminates, and we return a nullptr on line 14.

2.3.3.4   MAKEEMPTY

The MakeEmpty member function is designed to remove all items in the list. Thus, we use the same "step through" technique described in GetItem, but this time, we delete the nodes as we go along, and ultimately set the mHead equal to nullptr, which indicates an empty list.

```
1    void UnorderedList::MakeEmpty()
2    {
3            Node* temp = nullptr;
4
5            while(mHead != nullptr)
6            {
7                    temp = mHead;
8                    mHead = mHead->mNext;
9                    delete temp;
10           }
11   }
```

In this member function, unlike the GetItem member function, we *do* want to modify the list's structure by systematically removing all the elements in the list. Thus, we can use mHead to move through the list. However, we still keep a temp pointer, because for each node, we keep track of the current mHead with temp (line 7), then we progress mHead forward in the list, by making it point to the next item in the list (line 8), and finally we delete the previous mHead (held by temp) on line 9.

Note that we *know* mHead will equal nullptr by the time we exit the loop (because it is the loop termination condition, in the header of the while loop.) Thus, we have successfully set the mHead to nullptr and satisfied the condition that an empty list's mHead points to nullptr.

2.3.3.5   INSERT

```
1    void UnorderedList::InsertItem(int item)
2    {
3          //create new node
4          Node* node = new Node();
5
6          node->mData = item;
7          node->mNext = mHead;    //set next to *current* mHead
8
9          mHead = node;   //now the NEW node is the new mHead
10   }
```

The Insert method is fairly straightforward. When we want to add a node to our list, we first create the node in memory, completely separate from the list (line 4.) Then, we set the node's mData member to the item passed in (line 6.)

The crucial part of not losing the rest of the list is on line 7. Since this newly created node (named node at this point) is to be the new head of the list, which means the current head of the list must be pointed to by this new node's mNext.

And finally, we establish the new node we just created as the new head of the list on line 9.

Note that there is a bug in the above code. This bug would present itself if we ran out of memory. How would you remedy the problem? *Hint: Use* isFull().

2.3.3.6   REMOVEITEM

If you spend any significant time in computer science, software engineering, or related fields, you will find that manipulating the structure of data structures can be a challenge. In many cases, removing an item from a data structure is the most difficult operation. This is the case with our unordered linked list.

Let's look at the code and then I'll explain why we go through a little more trouble. It's straightforward if you sit down and really think about what the code is doing.

```
1    void UnorderedList::RemoveItem(int item)
2    {
3          Node* temp = mHead;
4          Node* holder = nullptr;
5
6          if(mHead != nullptr)
7          {
8                //special case:  mHead is the node we want.
9                if(mHead->mData == item)
10               {
11                     temp = mHead;
12                     mHead = mHead->mNext;
13                     delete temp;
14               }
15               else
16               {
17                     //other cases - check the "next"
18                     while(temp != nullptr && temp->mNext != nullptr)
19                     {
20                           if(temp->mNext->mData == item)
21                           {
22                                 holder = temp->mNext;
23                                 temp->mNext = temp->mNext->mNext;
24                                 delete holder;
25                                 break;
26                           }
27
28                           temp = temp->mNext;
29                     }//end while
30               }
31          }
32   }
```

At the beginning of this code, on lines 3 and 4, we declare two Node pointer variables. The variable temp is used to walk through the list as we search for the item to remove. The variable holder is used if we find the item we wish to remove. We use it to hold that node while we restructure the list (line 23.)

The first thing we do is check to ensure that the head of the list is not null (line 7.) If the head were null, we know we're not going to find the item in question because our list is empty. This is also required because we access data within the head of the list, and if you tried accessing any of the data members of a `nullptr`, it will cause a runtime error.

There are two cases we take into account. The first is on line 9-14. This is if the node we want is the head of the list. We capture the current head (line 11) and then set the `mHead` equal to the `mNext` node (line 12), and finally delete the old head (line 13.)

The typical case is that the node is not the head, and this is handled on lines 15-30. On line 18, we ensure firstly that the `temp` pointer isn't null itself, and then use && to check if the `mNext` of temp is `nullptr`. You might wonder how we can do this. Won't the program crash if temp is nullptr and we perform the check on `temp->mNext`? Normally this would be the case, but I'm making use of a really cool feature in C++ and many programming languages called **short circuiting**. If you recall your basic Boolean logic – *both* operands of a logical AND operator (`&&`) must be true for the whole statement to be `true`, right? Well, with C++ and many other languages, if the first operand is found to be `false`, the code doesn't even bother checking the code after the `&&` statement because no matter what, the whole statement will be `false`. Clever, eh? So no crashing will occur. Note that the order does matter. If you switched the order of the operands of `&&`, you would eventually incur the wrath of a very angry program crashing.

Line 20 checks and determines if we've found the item we're looking for. If we have, we capture the current `temp->mNext` on line 22, then we bypass the node we're about to remove by setting `temp`'s `mNext` to `temp->mNext->mNext` on line 23. Finally, on 24 and 25, we delete the node we need to remove and then break out of the loop.

2.3.3.7   PRINTLIST

This member function is a utility function to make viewing the list easier. It is not a very commonly found member function in implementations of UnorderedLists. However, this makes our lives easier, and there are a wide variety of UnorderedList implementations. I think you'll find it useful.

```cpp
void UnorderedList::PrintList()
{
        Node* temp = mHead;

        while(temp != nullptr)
        {
                cout<<temp->mData<<endl;
                temp = temp->mNext;
        }//end while
}
```

This member function uses a similar technique to our `GetItem` function. We loop through the list and print out each node as we come across it.

2.4   FULL SOURCE LISTING

2.4.1   UNORDEREDLIST.H

```cpp
class Node
{
public:
        int mData;
        Node* mNext;
};
```

```
7
8     class UnorderedList
9     {
10    public:
11          UnorderedList();
12          ~UnorderedList();
13          bool IsFull() const;
14          bool IsEmpty() const;
15          Node* GetItem(int item);
16          void MakeEmpty();
17          void InsertItem(int item);
18          void RemoveItem(int item);
19          void PrintList();
20    private:
21          Node* mHead;
22
23    };
```

2.4.2   UNOREDEDLIST.CPP

```
1     #include "UnorderedList.h"
2     #include <new>  //for bad_alloc
3     #include <iostream>
4     using namespace std;
5
6     UnorderedList::UnorderedList()
7     {
8           mHead = nullptr;
9     }
10
11    UnorderedList::~UnorderedList()
12    {
13          MakeEmpty();
14    }
15
16    bool UnorderedList::IsFull() const
17    {
18          try
19          {
20                Node* temp;
21                temp = new Node();
22                delete temp;
23                return false;
24          }
25          catch(bad_alloc ex)
```

```
26              {
27                      return true;
28              }
29    }
30
31    bool UnorderedList::IsEmpty() const
32    {
33            return mHead == nullptr;   //NULL if pre-C++ 11
34    }
35
36    Node* UnorderedList::GetItem(int item)
37    {
38            Node* temp = mHead;
39
40            while(temp!= nullptr)   //NULL if pre-C++ 11
41            {
42                    if(temp->mData = item)
43                    {
44                            return temp;
45                    }
46                    temp = temp->mNext;   //go to the next one
47            }
48
49        return nullptr;   //if never found, nust return NULL or
50    nullptr
51    }
52
53    void UnorderedList::MakeEmpty()
54    {
55            Node* temp = nullptr;
56
57            while(mHead != nullptr)
58            {
59                    temp = mHead;
60                    mHead = mHead->mNext;
61                    delete temp;
62            }
63    }
64
65    void UnorderedList::InsertItem(int item)
66    {
67            //create new node
68            Node* node = new Node();
69
70            node->mData = item;
71            node->mNext = mHead;   //set next to *current* mHead
72
73            mHead = node;   //now the NEW node is the new mHead
74    }
75
76    void UnorderedList::RemoveItem(int item)
```

```
77  {
78          Node* temp = mHead;
79          Node* holder = nullptr;
80
81          if(mHead != nullptr)
82          {
83                  //special case:  mHead is the node we want.
84                  if(mHead->mData == item)
85                  {
86                          temp = mHead;
87                          mHead = mHead->mNext;
88                          delete temp;
89                  }
90                  else
91                  {
92                          //other cases - check the "next"
93                          while(temp != nullptr && temp->mNext != nullptr)
94                          {
95                                  if(temp->mNext->mData == item)
96                                  {
97                                          holder = temp->mNext;
98                                          temp->mNext = temp->mNext->mNext;
99                                          delete holder;
100                                         break;
101                                 }
102
103                                 temp = temp->mNext;
104                         }//end while
105                 }
106         }
107 }
108
109 void UnorderedList::PrintList()
110 {
111         Node* temp = mHead;
112
113         while(temp != nullptr)
114         {
115                 cout<<temp->mData<<endl;
116                 temp = temp->mNext;
117         }//end while
118 }
```

2.4.3   MAIN.CPP – A SAMPLE DRIVER PROGRAM

```cpp
1   #include <iostream>
2   #include "UnorderedList.h"
3   using namespace std;
4
5   int main()
6   {
7         UnorderedList* ul = new UnorderedList();
8
9         ul->InsertItem(15);
10        ul->InsertItem(25);
11        ul->InsertItem(45);
12
13        ul->PrintList();
14
15        cout<<endl;
16
17        ul->RemoveItem(15);
18        ul->RemoveItem(25);
19
20        ul->PrintList();
21        cout<<endl;
22
23        ul->RemoveItem(45);
24
25        ul->PrintList();
26
27        ul->InsertItem(1);
28        ul->InsertItem(10);
29        ul->InsertItem(100);
30
31        ul->PrintList();
32        ul->RemoveItem(100);
33        cout<<endl;
34        ul->PrintList();
35
36
37        delete ul;
38        return 0;
39  }
```

Output from the above code:

```
45
25
15

45

100
10
1

10
1
Press any key to continue . . .
```

CHAPTER 3:
ORDERED LINKED LISTS

3.1   INTRODUCTION TO ORDERED LINKED LISTS

In this chapter, we'll take our study of linked structures further. With the UnorderedList we saw in the last chapter, we didn't have to be concerned with the order of the items as we inserted them into the list. But what if we want to maintain a sorted list of items? No matter what order we add the items to the list, what if we need to keep it in ascending or descending order?

This is what this chapter is concerned with – the **Ordered List** or **Sorted List** abstract data type. As with the last chapter, we are focusing on the linked representation of the list.

3.2   CONCEPTUAL OVERVIEW

To implement a linked list, we need to create two classes:

- The Node class
    - This represents an individual item in the list
    - Has a data part, containing the data that is to be stored in the node
    - Has a pointer to the next item in the list, so it can be joined into the list
    - Since it is so simple, many programmers just implement the Node as a struct instead of a class
- The OrderedList class
    - This represents a collection of Nodes, linked together in a sorted manner
    - Contains a special pointer to the beginning of the list, called the **head** of the list
        - In the example of an ascending sorted list, the head will always be the smallest item in the list

How the nodes connect with one another is essentially the same as with the unordered linked list. However, we now must concern ourselves with inserting a node into the correct place.

3.2.1   THE NODE CLASS

This class is identical to the node class we had before. It has two public data members.

Data Member Name	Data Type	Description
mData	int	This data member of the Node class will hold the actual data that the list is trying to maintain. Each node holds a single integer.
mNext	Node*	This data member of the Node class is a *pointer* to another Node object. Specifically, in terms of how we are going to use it, it will point to the very next item in the linked list.

3.2.2   THE ORDEREDLIST CLASS

This class is going to be a full-fledged, encapsulated class. We have to determine what data we're going to maintain as private data members of the class, and what member functions we want to operate on the class.

First, the data member

Data Member Name	Data Type	Description
mHead	Node*	This data member points to the head of the list. When there are no Nodes in the list, mHead points to nullptr. Since each node points to the next node in the list, the list will be relatively self-structuring as we define the

		member functions

Now, the member functions

Member Function Name	Return type	Parameters	Description
OrderedList	None (constructor)	None	This will initialize the list by setting the `mHead` variable to `nullptr`. Thus, the list starts empty.
~OrderedList	None (destructor)	None	This will indirectly make the list empty again, removing all elements that are currently in the list, one at a time.
IsFull	bool	None	This returns if the list is full or not. In the case of a list that keeps creating nodes on the heap, you might think it would never be full. But this isn't the case. If there is no memory left, then the list is full. More on how we test if there's no memory left later.
IsEmpty	bool	None	This returns if the list is empty. In other words, does the `mHead` variable point to `nullptr`?
GetItem	Node*	`int item`	Returns a pointer to an object in the list if the `item` is found. Returns `nullptr` otherwise.
MakeEmpty	void	None	Makes the list empty.

			Removes all elements from the list.
InsertItem	void	`int item`	Inserts the item into the list in a sorted manner (ascending.)
RemoveItem	void	`int item`	Removes the item specified as a parameter if it exists.
PrintList	void	None	Prints the contents of the list

3.3   ORDEREDLIST IMPLEMENTATION

File	Type	Description
main.cpp	C++ File (.cpp)	This is the *driver* file that we will use to test our class out.
OrderedList.h	Header File (.h)	This is the specification file of our `OrderedList`. We will also define the `Node` type in here.
OrderedList.cpp	C++ File (.cpp)	This is the implementation file of our `OrderedList`. We will implement the actual functions in here.

3.3.1 ORDEREDLIST SPECIFICATION FILE (.H)

The specification file is pretty much exactly what we expect. We have the same method signatures as our UnorderedList (except obviously, the constructors will be different.)

```
1   class Node
2   {
3   public:
4       int mData;
5       Node* mNext;
6   };
7
8   class OrderedList
9   {
10  public:
11      OrderedList();
12      ~OrderedList();
13      bool IsFull() const;
14      bool IsEmpty() const;
15      Node* GetItem(int item);
16      void MakeEmpty();
17      void InsertItem(int item);
18      void RemoveItem(int item);
19      void PrintList();
20  private:
21      Node* mHead;
22
23  };
```

3.3.2 ORDEREDLIST MEMBER FUNCTION IMPLEMENTATIONS

All member functions are identical to the UnorderedList, except for Insert, which I define in this section.

Note that changing this one member function changes the entire structure of how the linked list is maintained. We end up with a list that will keep the data in ascending order. This takes a little bit of extra work, but is relatively straightforward when you sit down and think through the different scenarios.

3.3.2.1   INSERT

```
1    void OrderedList::InsertItem(int item)
2    {
3            Node* newNode = new Node();
4            newNode->mData = item;
5
6            Node* walker = mHead;
7
8
9            if(mHead == nullptr)
10           {
11                   newNode->mNext = nullptr;
12                   mHead = newNode;
13           }
14           else if(newNode->mData < mHead->mData)
15           {
16                   //insert before current head
17                   newNode->mNext = mHead;
18                   mHead = newNode;
19           }
20           else
21           {
22                   while(walker->mNext != nullptr)
23                   {
24                           if(newNode->mData < walker->mNext->mData)
25                           {
26                                   break;
27                           }
28
29                           walker = walker->mNext;
30                   }//end while
31
32                   newNode->mNext = walker->mNext;
33                   walker->mNext = newNode;
34           }
35    }
```

This code may look a little bit complicated, but there are three major cases we divide the code into via use of `if-else` selection statements. The three special cases are:

- `mHead` is equal to `nullptr`
  - Lines 9 - 13
  - This means our new node is the *first* node to be inserted into the list
- The `newNode`'s `mData` is less than the data in the head of the list
  - Lines 14 - 19
  - This means we have to put our new node *before* the head, and make our new node the new head
- Otherwise,
  - Lines 20 - 34
  - We move through the list with a `walker` variable
  - When we find data from the `walker`'s `mNext` that is greater than our new node's data, we know this is the place to put the new node

The lines 22-30 might take a little bit more explanation. As long as the `walker->mNext` is not `nullptr`, we check if the new node's data is less than the `walker`'s (lines 24-27.) If it is, we break out of the loop. Regardless, after the loop, we set the newNode->mNext equal to `walker->mNext` on line 32. This is so we don't lose the rest of the list. Then, we set `walker->mNext` equal to our `newNode` on line 33. This links the two separate linked lists fully together.

Here are a couple illustrations to help clarify what's going on in this third case, which is arguably the most complex.

Let's say we're trying to insert a 20 in the middle of a node with 15, and a node with 25.

After we create the node, the list and our "free floating" node look like this:

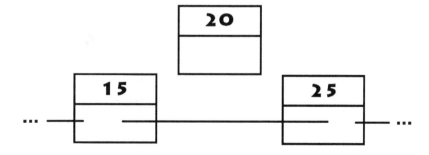

The mData of each node is indicated by the number in the top part of the node, and the mNext is indicated by the lines linking each node. Note that the … simply indicates there could be an arbitrary number of other nodes in the list on either side of the nodes we're looking at.

Lines 32 and 33 are:

```
newNode->mNext = walker->mNext;
walker->mNext = newNode;
```

Line 32 causes us to link our new node into the list on the right side, as thus:

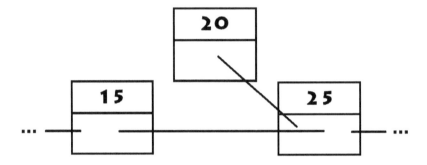

Now, we must connect our new node into the list from the left side, meaning the node with 15 (in our example) must set its mNext equal to our new node, breaking the direct link it has with the node containing 25. The code for this is on line 33, as restated above, where we set the mNext of our walker (the node with 15 in this example) to our newNode.

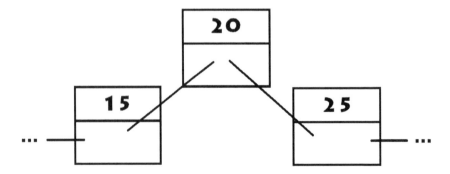

Thus, our new node falls in line with the other nodes.

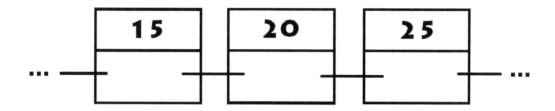

Note that, as with our UnorderedList, there is a bug in the above code. This bug would present itself if we ran out of memory. How would you remedy the problem? *Hint: Use* `isFull()`.

3.4 FULL SOURCE LISTING

3.4.1 ORDEREDLIST.H

```
1    class Node
2    {
3    public:
4          int mData;
5          Node* mNext;
6    };
7
8    class OrderedList
9    {
10   public:
11         OrderedList();
12         ~OrderedList();
13         bool IsFull() const;
14         bool IsEmpty() const;
15         Node* GetItem(int item);
```

```
16          void MakeEmpty();
17          void InsertItem(int item);
18          void RemoveItem(int item);
19          void PrintList();
20   private:
21          Node* mHead;
22
23   };
```

3.4.2   ORDEREDLIST.CPP

```
1    #include "OrderedList.h"
2    #include <new>
3    #include <iostream>
4    using namespace std;
5
6    OrderedList::OrderedList()
7    {
8           mHead = nullptr;
9    }
10
11   OrderedList::~OrderedList()
12   {
13          MakeEmpty();
14   }
15
16   bool OrderedList::IsFull() const
17   {
18          try
19          {
20                 Node* temp;
21                 temp = new Node();
22                 delete temp;
23                 return false;
24          }
25          catch(bad_alloc ex)
26          {
27                 return true;
28          }
29   }
30
31   bool OrderedList::IsEmpty() const
32   {
33          return mHead == nullptr;
34   }
35
36   void OrderedList::MakeEmpty()
```

```
37    {
38            Node* temp = nullptr;
39
40            while(mHead != nullptr)
41            {
42                    temp = mHead;
43                    mHead = mHead->mNext;
44                    delete temp;
45            }
46    }
47
48    void OrderedList::InsertItem(int item)
49    {
50            Node* newNode = new Node();
51            newNode->mData = item;
52
53            Node* walker = mHead;
54
55
56            if(mHead == nullptr)
57            {
58                    newNode->mNext = nullptr;
59                    mHead = newNode;
60            }
61            else if(newNode->mData < mHead->mData)
62            {
63                    //insert before current head
64                    newNode->mNext = mHead;
65                    mHead = newNode;
66            }
67            else
68            {
69                    while(walker->mNext != nullptr)
70                    {
71                            if(newNode->mData < walker->mNext->mData)
72                            {
73                                    break;
74                            }
75
76                            walker = walker->mNext;
77                    }//end while
78
79                    newNode->mNext = walker->mNext;
80                    walker->mNext = newNode;
81            }
82    }
83
84    void OrderedList::RemoveItem(int item)
85    {
86            Node* temp = mHead;
87            Node* holder = nullptr;
```

```
88
89          if(mHead != nullptr)
90          {
91                  //special case:  mHead is the node we want.
92                  if(mHead->mData == item)
93                  {
94                          temp = mHead;
95                          mHead = mHead->mNext;
96                          delete temp;
97                  }
98                  else
99                  {
100                         //other cases - check the "next"
101                         while(temp != nullptr && temp->mNext != nullptr)
102                         {
103                                 if(temp->mNext->mData == item)
104                                 {
105                                         holder = temp->mNext;
106                                         temp->mNext = temp->mNext->mNext;
107                                         delete holder;
108                                         break;
109                                 }
110
111                                 temp = temp->mNext;
112                         }//end while
113                 }
114         }
115 }
116
117 void OrderedList::PrintList()
118 {
119         Node* temp = mHead;
120
121         while(temp != nullptr)
122         {
123                 cout<<temp->mData<<endl;
124                 temp = temp->mNext;
125         }//end while
126 }
```

3.4.3   MAIN.CPP – A SAMPLE DRIVER PROGRAM

```
1    #include <iostream>
2    #include "OrderedList.h"
3    using namespace std;
```

```
4
5    int main()
6    {
7          OrderedList* ol = new OrderedList();
8
9          ol->InsertItem(15);
10         ol->InsertItem(25);
11         ol->InsertItem(20);
12         ol->InsertItem(7);
13         ol->InsertItem(4);
14         ol->InsertItem(150);
15         ol->InsertItem(75);
16         ol->InsertItem(155);
17         ol->InsertItem(160);
18         ol->InsertItem(157);
19
20         ol->PrintList();
21         cout<<endl;
22
23         ol->RemoveItem(150);
24         ol->RemoveItem(4);
25         ol->RemoveItem(160);
26         ol->RemoveItem(20);
27
28         ol->InsertItem(200);
29         ol->InsertItem(5);
30
31         ol->PrintList();
32
33         return 0;
34   }
```

Output from the source code above:

```
4
7
15
20
25
75
150
155
157
160

5
7
15
```

```
25
75
155
157
200
Press any key to continue . . .
```

CHAPTER 4:
STACKS

4.1 INTRODUCTION TO STACKS

In this chapter, we explore another fundamental data structure – the stack ADT. A **stack** is an abstract data type in which elements are added (**pushed**) and removed (**popped**) from one end, namely the **top** of the stack. Because of this, we call a stack a **last in, first out (LIFO)** data structure. This is because the last item you pushed onto the stack is the first one that will come off the stack when popped.

4.2 CONCEPTUAL OVERVIEW

Stacks are a frequently used data structure in computer science. One major use for stacks is to keep track of function calls. If the main function calls function A, then A calls B, when B finishes, control returns to A, and then when A finishes, control returns to B.

Visually, it looks something like the following:

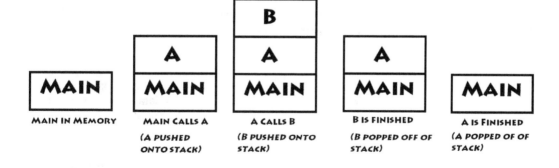

In a program, this stack is called the **call stack** or **function call stack**. It's a pretty straightforward and self-descriptive name.

4.2.1   THE NODE CLASS

This class is identical to the Node class we have used before. I will re-write it here just for the sake of review, or if you're focusing solely on this chapter. It has two public data members.

Data Member Name	Data Type	Description
mData	int	This data member of the Node class will hold the actual data that the list is trying to maintain. Each node holds a single integer.
mNext	Node*	This data member of the Node class is a *pointer* to another Node object. Specifically, in terms of how we are going to use it, it will point to the very next lower item in the stack.

4.2.2   THE STACK CLASS

First, we look at the data member. Note that the name has changed. Although we still use a similar linked structure as with our list examples, there are some subtle, but important difference.

Data Member Name	Data Type	Description
mTop	Node*	This data member points to the top of the stack. When there are no Nodes in the stack, mTop points to nullptr. Each node in the stack points to the node below it, or if it's the node on

		the bottom of the stack, it will point to `nullptr`.

Secondly, let's look at the member functions of the `Stack` class. For the sake of simplicity, just as with previous data structure examples, we're going to maintain integers in our nodes, but you could use essentially any other data type, or even code the stack generically using class templates.

Member Function Name	Return type	Parameters	Description
Stack	None (constructor)	None	This will initialize the stack by setting the `mTop` variable to `nullptr`. Thus, the stack starts empty.
~Stack	None (destructor)	None	This will indirectly make the stack empty again, removing all elements currently in the stack, one at a time.
IsFull	bool	None	Returns `true` if the stack is full, and `false` if the stack is not full.
IsEmpty	bool	None	Returns `true` if the stack is empty, and `false` if it is not empty.
Push	void	int item	Pushes (adds) an item to the stack, if the stack is not full.
Pop	int	None	Pops the top of the stack (removes the top) and returns the value of that item if the stack is not empty
Top	int	None	Returns the top of the stack without removing it

MakeEmpty	void	None	Pops all items off the stack.
PrintStack	Void	None	Prints the contents of the stack

4.3   STACK IMPLEMENTATION

File	Type	Description
main.cpp	C++ File (.cpp)	This is the *driver* file that we will use to test our class out.
Stack.h	Header File (.h)	This is the specification file of our Stack. We will also define the Node type in here.
Stack.cpp	C++ File (.cpp)	This is the implementation file of our Stack. We will implement the actual functions in here.

4.3.1   STACK SPECIFICATION FILE (.H)

```
1   class Node
2   {
3   public:
4         int mData;
5         Node* mNext;
6   };
7
8   class Stack
9   {
10  public:
11        Stack();
12        ~Stack();
13        bool isFull() const;
14        bool isEmpty() const;
15        void Push(int item);
16        int Pop();
17        int Top() const;
18        void MakeEmpty();
```

```
19          void PrintStack();
20
21  private:
            Node* mTop;
    };
```

4.3.2 STACK MEMBER FUNCTION IMPLEMENTATIONS

Some of the member functions should look very familiar, because they haven't really changed from our list implementations in earlier chapters.

4.3.2.1   CONSTRUCTOR AND DESTRUCTOR

```
1  Stack::Stack()
2  {
3        mTop = nullptr;
4  }
5
6  Stack::~Stack()
7  {
8        MakeEmpty();
9  }
```

4.3.2.2   ISFULL AND ISEMPTY

```
1   bool Stack::isFull() const
2   {
3         try
4         {
5               Node* temp;
6               temp = new Node();
7               delete temp;
8               return false;
9         }
10        catch(bad_alloc ex)
11        {
12              return true;
```

```
13              }
14    }
15
16    bool Stack::isEmpty() const
17    {
18              return mTop == nullptr;
19    }
```

4.3.2.3   PUSH

When we think of how we're going to push items onto the stack, we note that each new item we add onto the stack becomes the new top of the stack. That means when we create a new node to go on top of the stack that we must point the new node's mNext to the current mTop of the stack, and then set the new node *as* the new mTop.

Although the best implementation would not include print statements, but instead would include exceptions, we're more concerned with focusing on the stack ADT, not exception handling at this point.

```
1     void Stack::Push(int item)
2     {
3            if(!isFull())
4            {
5                   Node* newNode = new Node();
6
7                   newNode->mData = item;
8                   newNode->mNext = mTop;
9                   mTop = newNode;
10
11
12            }
13            else
14            {
15                   cout<<"Cannot push onto a full stack!"<<endl;
16                   //you could throw an exception here too
17            }
18
19    }
```

We check to see if the stack is full on line 3, since we cannot push onto a full stack. If the stack isn't full, we can add a node to the stack. We create the node in memory on line 5. Then, we set its data on line 7. Then, we prepare to become the new top. So as not to lose the rest of the stack, we set the `newNode->mNext` equal to the current `mTop` on line 8. Finally, on line 9, we establish the newly added node as the new `mTop`.

Lines 13-17 handle the case that the stack *is* full. If this is the case, in this particular implementation, we just print out a warning. Note that the value returned by the function in this scenario would be 0, which is a valid value. To avoid this, you could use exception handling and throw an exception if the stack is full.

4.3.2.4   POP

To pop an item off of the stack, you save the current top of the stack with a temporary node. You also must save the value that is in the top node, if your implementation returns the value to the user. Note that some implementations have `Pop` as a `void` function, which does not return a value.

```
1    int Stack::Pop()
2    {
3          int retVal = 0;
4
5          if(!isEmpty())
6          {
7                Node* temp = mTop;
8
9                mTop = mTop->mNext;
10               retVal = temp->mData;
11               delete temp;
12         }
13         else
14         {
15               cout<<"Cannot pop off of an empty stack!"<<endl;
16               //you could throw an exception here too
17         }
18
19         return retVal;
20
21   }
```

In this implementation, we check to see if the stack is empty on line 5, and then, if it is, we temporarily maintain the address of the current top of the stack (line 7.) Then, we progress the top to the next item in the stack (line 9), grab the return value of the item we are about to delete (line 10), and finally delete the `temp` variable, which holds the previous `mTop` value.

On lines 13-17, we handle the case if we try to pop off of an empty stack. In this implementation, we simply print a message out to the user. Finally, on line 19, we return the value we obtained from the previous top (or, the value will simply be 0, the value it was initialized at, if the stack was empty.)

4.3.2.5 TOP

The Top member function has striking similarities to the Pop member function, but it is non-destructive, that is, it doesn't change the structure of the stack.

```
int Stack::Top() const
{
        int retVal = 0;

        if(!isEmpty())
        {
                retVal = mTop->mData;
        }
        else
        {
                cout<<"The Stack is empty!"<<endl;
                //you could throw an exception here too
        }

        return retVal;
}
```

4.3.2.6 MAKEEMPTY

Conceptually, `MakeEmpty` is not much different, except for variable names, from previous versions of this member function that we saw in our list implementations. However, we do take advantage of the fact that we can simply say as long as the stack isn't empty (by using `isEmpty`), we `Pop` (which removes items from the stack.

```
void Stack::MakeEmpty()
{
        while(!isEmpty())
        {
```

```
        Pop();
    }
}
```

4.3.2.7   PRINTSTACK

Again, like the `PrintList` counterparts, `PrintStack` simply moves through the stack and prints each item in the stack in a non-destructive manner.

```
1   void Stack::PrintStack()
2   {
3          Node* temp = mTop;
4
5          while(temp != nullptr)
6          {
7                  cout<<temp->mData<<endl;
8                  temp = temp->mNext;
9          }
10  }
```

4.4   FULL SOURCE LISTING

4.4.1 STACK.H

```
1    class Node
2    {
3    public:
4           int mData;
5           Node* mNext;
6    };
7
8    class Stack
9    {
10   public:
11          Stack();
12          ~Stack();
13          bool isFull() const;
```

```
14          bool isEmpty() const;
15          void Push(int item);
16          int Pop();
17          int Top() const;
18          void MakeEmpty();
19          void PrintStack();
20   private:
21          Node* mTop;
22   };
```

4.4.2 STACK.CPP

```
1    #include "Stack.h"
2    #include <new>
3    #include <iostream>
4    using namespace std;
5
6    Stack::Stack()
7    {
8           mTop = nullptr;
9    }
10
11   Stack::~Stack()
12   {
13          MakeEmpty();
14   }
15
16
17   bool Stack::isFull() const
18   {
19          try
20          {
21                 Node* temp;
22                 temp = new Node();
23                 delete temp;
24                 return false;
25          }
26          catch(bad_alloc ex)
27          {
28                 return true;
29          }
30   }
31
32   bool Stack::isEmpty() const
33   {
```

```
34          return mTop == nullptr;
35     }
36
37     void Stack::Push(int item)
38     {
39          if(!isFull())
40          {
41               Node* newNode = new Node();
42
43               newNode->mData = item;
44               newNode->mNext = mTop;
45               mTop = newNode;
46
47
48          }
49          else
50          {
51               cout<<"Cannot push onto a full stack!"<<endl;
52               //you could throw an exception here too
53          }
54
55     }
56
57     int Stack::Pop()
58     {
59          int retVal = 0;
60
61          if(!isEmpty())
62          {
63               Node* temp = mTop;
64
65               mTop = mTop->mNext;
66               retVal = temp->mData;
67               delete temp;
68          }
69          else
70          {
71               cout<<"Cannot pop off of an empty stack!"<<endl;
72               //you could throw an exception here too
73          }
74
75          return retVal;
76
77     }
78
79     int Stack::Top() const
80     {
81          int retVal = 0;
82
83          if(!isEmpty())
84          {
```

```
85              retVal = mTop->mData;
86          }
87          else
88          {
89                  cout<<"The Stack is empty!"<<endl;
90                  //you could throw an exception here too
91          }
92
93          return retVal;
94  }
95
96  void Stack::MakeEmpty()
97  {
98          while(!isEmpty())
99          {
100                 Pop();
101         }
102 }
103
104 void Stack::PrintStack()
105 {
106         Node* temp = mTop;
107
108         while(temp != nullptr)
109         {
110                 cout<<temp->mData<<endl;
111                 temp = temp->mNext;
112         }
113 }
```

4.4.3 MAIN.CPP – A SAMPLE DRIVER PROGRAM

```
1   #include <iostream>
2   #include "Stack.h"
3   using namespace std;
4
5   int main()
6   {
7           Stack myStack;
8
9           myStack.Push(10);
10          myStack.Push(15);
11          myStack.Push(12);
12          myStack.Push(100);
13          myStack.Push(50);
```

```
14
15          myStack.PrintStack();
16          cout<<endl;
17
18          myStack.Pop();
19          myStack.Pop();
20
21          myStack.PrintStack();
22          cout<<endl;
23
24          myStack.Push(500);
25          myStack.Push(45);
26
27          while(!myStack.isEmpty())
28          {
29                  cout<<myStack.Pop()<<endl;
30          }
31
32          //pop on empty stack
33          myStack.Pop();
34          return 0;
35  }
```

Output from the source code above:

```
50
100
12
15
10

12
15
10

45
500
12
15
10
Cannot pop off of an empty stack!
Press any key to continue . . .
```

CHAPTER 5:
QUEUES

5.1   INTRODUCTION TO QUEUES

The **queue** (pronounced "Cue" like the letter "Q" in English) is another very commonly used abstract data type. A queue is a **first in, first out (FIFO)** data structure. When we add an item to a queue, this operation is called **enqueue** (pronounced "in cue"), and when we remove an item from the queue, we call this operation **dequeue** (pronounced "dee cue".)

5.2   CONCEPTUAL OVERVIEW

The queue is arguably a little bit more complicated than the previous data structures we have described, because it maintains both a **rear** and a **front**. A queue can be thought of as a lunch line at a cafeteria or a line at a grocery store. Customers enter the rear of the line (queue) and exit out the front of the line (queue.)

5.2.1   THE NODE CLASS

Our trusty Node class is back to help us in our journey into queues. It has two public data members as before.

Data Member Name	Data Type	Description
mData	int	This data member of the Node class will hold the actual data that the list is trying to maintain. Each node holds a single integer.
mNext	Node*	This data member of the

		Node class is a *pointer* to another Node object. Specifically, in terms of how we are going to use it, it will point to the very next item in the queue ahead of the current item.

5.2.2   THE QUEUE CLASS

First, let's take a look at the data members. In the case of the queue, there are not one, but *two*.

Data Member Name	Data Type	Description
mFront	Node*	This data member points to the front of the queue. When there are no Nodes in the stack, mFront points to nullptr, and so does mRear. Each node in the queue points to the node after it, or if it's the front of the queue, it points to nullptr. The front of the queue is where items are dequeued from.
mRear	Node*	This data member points to the rear of the queue. The rear is where items are enqueued to.

Now, let's take a look at the member functions of the Queue class. Once again, we use integers as the data we're maintaining.

Member Function Name	Return type	Parameters	Description
Queue	None (constructor)	None	This will initialize the stack by setting the `mFront` and `mRear` variables to `nullptr`. Thus, the queue starts empty.
~Queue	None (destructor)	None	This will indirectly make the queue empty again, removing all elements currently in the queue, one at a time.
IsFull	bool	None	Returns `true` if the queue is full, and `false` if it is not.
IsEmpty	bool	None	Returns true if the queue is empty, and false otherwise. Recall that an empty queue is one in which both the `mFront` and `mRear` of the queue are equal to `nullptr`.
Enqueue	void	int item	Enqueues (adds) an item to the queue, if the queue is not full.
Dequeue	int	None	Removes the item at the front of the queue, and returns that item, if the queue is not empty.
MakeEmpty	void	None	Removes all items from the queue.
PrintQueue	void	None	Print the elements in the queue, in order from the front to the

			rear.

5.3   QUEUE IMPLEMENTATION

File	Type	Description
main.cpp	C++ File (.cpp)	This is the *driver* file that we will use to test our class out.
Queue.h	Header File (.h)	This is the specification file of our Queue. We will also define the Node type in here.
Queue.cpp	C++ File (.cpp)	This is the implementation file of our Queue. We will implement the actual functions in here.

5.3.1   QUEUE SPECIFICATION FILE (.H)

```
1    class Node
2    {
3    public:
4            int mData;
5            Node* mNext;
6    };
7
8    class Queue
9    {
10   public:
11           Queue();
12           ~Queue();
13           bool isEmpty() const;
14           bool isFull() const;
15           void Enqueue(int item);
16           int Dequeue();
17           void MakeEmpty();
18           void PrintQueue();
19   private:
```

```
20          Node* mFront;
21          Node* mRear;
22    };
```

5.3.2   QUEUE MEMBER FUNCTION IMPLEMENTATIONS

Some of the member functions are essentially the same as what we've seen before in previous chapters.

5.3.2.1   CONSTRUCTOR AND DESTRUCTOR

```
1     Queue::Queue()
2     {
3           mFront = nullptr;
4           mRear = nullptr;
5     }
6
7     Queue::~Queue()
8     {
9           MakeEmpty();
10    }
```

In this implementation, note that we simply set *both* the front and the rear to the null pointer on lines 3 and 4, in the constructor. With queues, as mentioned earlier, we have to track two different pointers, not just one.

The destructor is really not any different than previous implementations of ADTs we've explored already. We simply let MakeEmpty do all the work.

5.3.2.2   ISFULL AND ISEMPTY

```
1     bool Queue::isFull() const
2     {
3           Node* temp;
4
5           try
6           {
```

```
7              temp = new Node();
8              delete temp;
9              return false;
10        }
11     catch(bad_alloc ex)
12     {
13              return true;
14        }
15  }
16
17  bool Queue::isEmpty() const
18  {
19          return mFront == nullptr;
20  }
```

For `isFull`, we do as we have done before. We see if we can reserve memory or not. If we can, we return `false`, if we cannot, an exception is thrown and thus we return `true` – that the queue is full.

For `isEmpty`, we simply return if the front of the queue is pointing to the null pointer or not, since this essentially defines if the queue is empty or not.

5.3.2.3   ENQUEUE

```
1   void Queue::Enqueue(int item)
2   {
3          if(!isFull())
4          {
5                  Node* newNode = new Node();
6                  newNode->mData = item;
7                  newNode->mNext = nullptr;
8
9                  if(mRear == nullptr)
10                 {
11                         mFront = newNode;
12                 }
13                 else
14                 {
15                         mRear->mNext = newNode;
16                 }
17
18                 mRear = newNode;
19
```

```
20            }
21        else
22        {
23                cout<<"Cannot add to a full queue!"<<endl;
24                //also, could throw an exception here
25        }
26  }
```

If the queue isn't full, we create a new node on line 5, and then set the data for that node on line 6. Then, we set the mNext of the new node to nullptr, since this node will be at the rear of the queue – remember that we *add* nodes to the queue in the rear.

Lines 9-12 are for the situation in which the current mRear pointer is pointing to nullptr. What does this mean? If the rear of the queue is the null pointer, then we know that this item we are adding is the *first* item to be added to the queue. Otherwise, if this node *isn't* the first node to be added to the queue, we set the current rear's mNext to the new node.

Regardless of whether the node we just added is the first to be added or not, we must make this new node the new mRear, since it's the new rear of the queue.

Let's look at what happens if we enqueue the values 15, 100, and 20.

Enqueue(15)

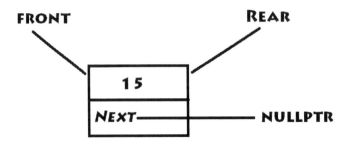

When there is only one item in the queue, we see that *both* the rear and front point to the node. The mNext points to the nullptr. Note that this particular addition of the first node would follow lines 9-12 in the code.

Enqueue(100)

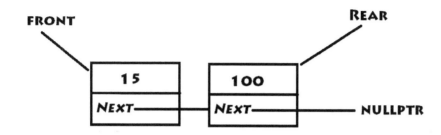

Enqueue(20)

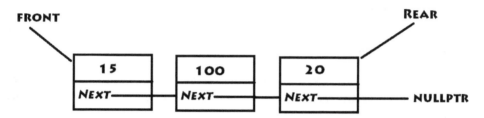

Notice that with all of the enqueue operations that are performed, the rear keeps changing, but except for the first node added to the queue, the front remains the same.

5.3.2.4   DEQUEUE

```
1    int Queue::Dequeue()
2    {
3         int retVal = 0;
4
5         if(!isEmpty())
6         {
7              Node* temp = mFront;
8              retVal = mFront->mData;
9              mFront = mFront->mNext;
10
11             if(mFront == nullptr)
12             {
```

```
13                    mRear = nullptr;
14                }
15                delete temp;
16           }
17       else
18       {
19                cout<<"Cannot remove from an empty queue!"<<endl;
20                //also, could throw an exception here
21       }
22
23       return retVal;
24  }
```

In the above code, we temporarily point to the current front of the queue, on line 7. On line 8, we obtain the data that we are to return. On line 9, we progress the front so the node that was behind it becomes the new front.

Lines 11-14 are to ensure if our new mFront variable is the nullptr, we know that the only way this happened is if we just dequeued the last node. Thus, we set the mRear variable to nullptr as well.

Regardless of which node we just deleted, we must delete the node that was the front previously, which we do on line 15.

Now, what does it look like if we call a dequeue on queue from earlier in the Enqueue section?

Dequeue( )

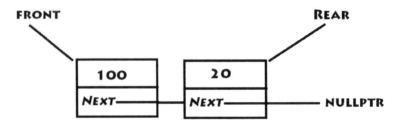

In this case, the first node we added, the one with 15 as its data, has been deleted. The front is now the next node in line (the one containing 100.) This is what we expect, since a queue is a FIFO data structure.

5.3.2.5   MAKEEMPTY

```
1   void Queue::MakeEmpty()
2   {
3         Node* temp;
4
5         while (mFront != nullptr)
6         {
7               temp = mFront;
8               mFront = mFront->mNext;
9               delete temp;
10        }//end while
11
12        mRear = nullptr;
13  }
```

The MakeEmpty member function is not *much* different front what we've seen before. We use a temp variable to point to the front at each iteration through the loop, until we come to the end of the queue (when the mFront is equal to nullptr.) Then, the additional step is to make mRear equal to nullptr.

5.3.2.6   PRINTQUEUE

```
1   void Queue::PrintQueue()
2   {
3         Node* temp = mFront;
4
5         while(temp != nullptr)
6         {
7               cout<<temp->mData<<endl;
8               temp = temp->mNext;
9         }
10  }
```

The printing function is of no surprise. We start at the front of the queue, and print the items in order from front to rear, which is how queues are ordered.

5.4   FULL SOURCE LISTING

5.4.1   QUEUE.H

```
1    class Node
2    {
3    public:
4          int mData;
5          Node* mNext;
6    };
7
8    class Queue
9    {
10   public:
11         Queue();
12         ~Queue();
13         bool isEmpty() const;
14         bool isFull() const;
15         void Enqueue(int item);
16         int Dequeue();
17         void MakeEmpty();
18         void PrintQueue();
19   private:
20         Node* mFront;
21         Node* mRear;
22   };
```

5.4.2   QUEUE.CPP

```
1    #include "Queue.h"
2    #include <iostream>
3    #include <new>
4    using namespace std;
5
6    Queue::Queue()
7    {
8          mFront = nullptr;
9          mRear = nullptr;
```

```
10    }
11
12    Queue::~Queue()
13    {
14          MakeEmpty();
15    }
16
17
18    bool Queue::isFull() const
19    {
20          Node* temp;
21
22          try
23          {
24                temp = new Node();
25                delete temp;
26                return false;
27          }
28          catch(bad_alloc ex)
29          {
30                return true;
31          }
32    }
33
34    bool Queue::isEmpty() const
35    {
36          return mFront == nullptr;
37    }
38
39    void Queue::Enqueue(int item)
40    {
41          if(!isFull())
42          {
43                Node* newNode = new Node();
44                newNode->mData = item;
45                newNode->mNext = nullptr;
46
47                if(mRear == nullptr)
48                {
49                      mFront = newNode;
50                }
51                else
52                {
53                      mRear->mNext = newNode;
54                }
55
56                mRear = newNode;
57
58          }
59          else
60          {
```

```
61              cout<<"Cannot add to a full queue!"<<endl;
62              //also, could throw an exception here
63          }
64  }
65
66  int Queue::Dequeue()
67  {
68          int retVal = 0;
69
70          if(!isEmpty())
71          {
72                  Node* temp = mFront;
73                  retVal = mFront->mData;
74                  mFront = mFront->mNext;
75
76                  if(mFront == nullptr)
77                  {
78                          mRear = nullptr;
79                  }
80                  delete temp;
81          }
82          else
83          {
84                  cout<<"Cannot remove from an empty queue!"<<endl;
85                  //also, could throw an exception here
86          }
87
88          return retVal;
89  }
90
91  void Queue::MakeEmpty()
92  {
93          Node* temp;
94
95          while (mFront != nullptr)
96          {
97                  temp = mFront;
98                  mFront = mFront->mNext;
99                  delete temp;
100         }//end while
101
102         mRear = nullptr;
103 }
104
105 void Queue::PrintQueue()
106 {
107         Node* temp = mFront;
108
109         while(temp != nullptr)
110         {
111                 cout<<temp->mData<<endl;
```

112	temp = temp->mNext;
113	}
114	}

5.4.3 MAIN.CPP – A SAMPLE DRIVER PROGRAM

```cpp
1   #include <iostream>
2   #include "Queue.h"
3   using namespace std;
4
5   int main()
6   {
7           Queue myQueue;
8
9           myQueue.Enqueue(100);
10          myQueue.Enqueue(150);
11          myQueue.Enqueue(25);
12          myQueue.Enqueue(170);
13
14          myQueue.PrintQueue();
15          cout<<endl;
16
17          myQueue.Dequeue();
18
19          myQueue.Enqueue(15);
20          myQueue.Dequeue();
21
22          myQueue.PrintQueue();
23          cout<<endl;
24
25          return 0;
26  }
```

Output from the source code above:

```
100
150
25
170

25
```

```
170
15

Press any key to continue . . .
```

CHAPTER 6:
SORTING

6.1   INTRODUCTION TO SORTING

Another very important topic that is often covered in second semester computer science courses is **sorting**. The basic problem is: we have a set of items, in an array for example, and they are out of order and we want them in order. There are many different sorting algorithms available, but knowing how to write them and how they work is important to you so you can become more proficient in the C++ programming language and begin to think about *how* to go about solving problems. Sorting algorithms just happen to be very useful both in practical applications as well as from a teaching perspective.

This is by no means an exhaustive text on the study of algorithm efficiency. However, I provide a very concise introduction here just so you can get an idea of what's going on. In **complexity analysis**, which is usually studied in more depth in a later computer science course, we are concerned with essentially how "fast" or "slow" an algorithm is, when we study the time it takes for this algorithm to execute. However, we cannot depend on a stopwatch because the same algorithm might perform very quickly on a high-performance gaming computer, and be several times slower on a netbook.

6.1.2   A VERY BRIEF INTRODUCTION TO COMPLEXITY ANALYSIS

Instead, we usually look at some input to the algorithm to determine how fast or slow it is. For example, let's assume we want to sort n elements. We concern ourselves with, in terms of the input size n, how quickly can we sort the elements, regardless of the machine we're on. To represent the relative speeds of algorithms, we put the algorithms into categories, called **complexity categories** or **complexity classes**. We use the so-called **Big-Oh** (or **Big-Omicron**) notation to describe different algorithmic categories.

If an algorithm, for example, responds independently of the input size, we say that algorithm is of **constant** complexity, notated as part of the category **O(1)**, read as "big oh of one". If another algorithm, say a linear search involves looking item by item through an array or list of some sort, we know that in the worst case, we go through *all n* of the items and don't find the item we're looking for. Thus, we say this has **linear** complexity, or **O(n)**. This doesn't mean that *every* time we run a linear search will be worse case – in fact, we *could* find the element to be the first element in the array. Instead, Big Oh provides an upper bound, or worst-case scenario.

Although much faster sorting algorithms exist, we concern ourselves with some of the slower (but easily implemented) sorting algorithms. These sorting algorithms fall into the complexity class **O(n^2)**, read as "big oh of n squared", also known as **quadratic** complexity.

6.1.3   A HANDY PRINT FUNCTION

A handy function to print the data in an array, so we don't have to write the code over and over again when checking the contents of an array is as follows.

```
1  void PrintArray(int arr[], int size)
2  {
3         for(int i = 0; i < size; i++)
4         {
5                 cout<<arr[i]<<endl;
6         }
7  }
```

6.2   BUBBLE SORT – A CLASSIC EXAMPLE OF EXCHANGE SORTS

Bubble sort is a classic sorting algorithm that is used frequently to teach the concepts behind a category of sorts known as **exchange sorts**. Exchange sorts are sorts that move through a list over and over again, exchanging elements that are out of order, until no out of order pairs exist in the list. This type of sort is considered impractical for all but very small lists, because these sorts make so many exchanges on average.

In fact, Bubble sort is an excellent teaching example, but is so impractical and inefficient that one of my professors at the University of Michigan – Dearborn gave it the nickname, "Lazy Student Sort", due to its easy implementation, but with complete lack of consideration for efficiency.

6.2.1   AN IMPLEMENTATION OF BUBBLESORT

There are different implementations of Bubble sort, but I offer the following for consideration.

```
1    void BubbleSort(int a[], int size)
2    {
3         bool swapped;
4         int temp = 0;
5
6         for(int i = 0; i < size; i++)
7         {
8              swapped = false;
9              for(int j = 1; j < size; j++)
10             {
11                  if(a[j-1] > a[j])
12                  {
13                       temp = a[j];
14                       a[j] = a[j-1];
15                       a[j-1] = temp;
16                       swapped = true;
17                  }
18             }//end inner loop
19             if(!swapped)
20             {
21                  break;   //exit outer loop
22             }
23        }//end outer loop
24   }
```

We use an outer loop, and an inner loop. As a slight consideration for efficiency's sake, we declare a Boolean variable named swapped on line 3. This variable is assigned the value false on line 8, as it prepares to go through another round of searching for out of order items

 If at least one out of order item is found, swapped is set to true, and therefore, the test condition and break statement on lines 19-22 will not be executed. However, if we go through the entire list and find no out of order items, that means they are all sorted, and thus swapped remains at its assigned value, false. So, the break on line 21 is executed, and we don't go through any more loops through the data than are necessary.

6.2.2   AN ENTIRE SOURCE FILE USING BUBBLESORT

```
1    #include <iostream>
2    using namespace std;
3
4    void BubbleSort(int arr[], int size);   //prototype
5    void PrintArray(int arr[], int size);
6    int main()
7    {
8          const int ARR_SIZE = 10;
9          int arr[ARR_SIZE] = {55, 6, 14, 40, 3, 1, 7, 10, 8, 24};
10
11         cout<<"Before sort:"<<endl;
12         PrintArray(arr, ARR_SIZE);
13         cout<<endl<<endl;
14
15         BubbleSort(arr, ARR_SIZE);
16
17         cout<<"Sorted:"<<endl;
18         PrintArray(arr, ARR_SIZE);
19
20         return 0;
21   }
22
23   void BubbleSort(int a[], int size)
24   {
25         bool swapped;
26         int temp = 0;
27
28         for(int i = 0; i < size; i++)
29         {
30               swapped = false;
31               for(int j = 1; j < size; j++)
32               {
33                     if(a[j-1] > a[j])
34                     {
35                           temp = a[j];
36                           a[j] = a[j-1];
37                           a[j-1] = temp;
38                           swapped = true;
39                     }
40               }//end inner loop
```

```
41              if(!swapped)
42              {
43                    break;   //exit outer loop
44              }
45         }//end outer loop
46  }
47
48  void PrintArray(int arr[], int size)
49  {
50         for(int i = 0; i < size; i++)
51         {
52                cout<<arr[i]<<endl;
53         }
54  }
```

The output of the above code is thus:

```
Before sort:
55
6
14
40
3
1
7
10
8
24


Sorted:
1
3
6
7
8
10
14
24
40
55
Press any key to continue . . .
```

6.2.3   A CLOSER LOOK AT THE ABOVE SORTING PROCESS

We start with the following unsorted list:

55   6   14   40   3   1   7   10   8   24

If we print out the list, following each swap that is performed in the inner loop, we have the following:

```
6 55 14 40 3 1 7 10 8 24
6 14 55 40 3 1 7 10 8 24
6 14 40 55 3 1 7 10 8 24
6 14 40 3 55 1 7 10 8 24
6 14 40 3 1 55 7 10 8 24
6 14 40 3 1 7 55 10 8 24
6 14 40 3 1 7 10 55 8 24
6 14 40 3 1 7 10 8 55 24
6 14 40 3 1 7 10 8 24 55

6 14 3 40 1 7 10 8 24 55
6 14 3 1 40 7 10 8 24 55
6 14 3 1 7 40 10 8 24 55
6 14 3 1 7 10 40 8 24 55
6 14 3 1 7 10 8 40 24 55
6 14 3 1 7 10 8 24 40 55

6 3 14 1 7 10 8 24 40 55
6 3 1 14 7 10 8 24 40 55
6 3 1 7 14 10 8 24 40 55
6 3 1 7 10 14 8 24 40 55
6 3 1 7 10 8 14 24 40 55

3 6 1 7 10 8 14 24 40 55
3 1 6 7 10 8 14 24 40 55
3 1 6 7 8 10 14 24 40 55

1 3 6 7 8 10 14 24 40 55
```

I've inserted a gap after each iteration of the inner loop has completed. You can see in the first line, the 55 and 6 have been swapped, because they were out of order. Then, as the index of the array increases, we see that the 14 and 55 are out of place so they too are swapped.

By the end of the first inner loop iteration, the 55 is at its rightful place at the end of the list. If you look carefully through the output from the first iteration, you can see that the 55 is progressively moved toward the top of the list. We call this "bubbling" the number up into its rightful place, hence why this sort is called Bubble sort.

```
55 6 14 40 3 1 7 10 8 24
6 55 14 40 3 1 7 10 8 24
6 14 55 40 3 1 7 10 8 24
6 14 40 55 3 1 7 10 8 24
6 14 40 3 55 1 7 10 8 24
6 14 40 3 1 55 7 10 8 24
6 14 40 3 1 7 55 10 8 24
6 14 40 3 1 7 10 55 8 24
6 14 40 3 1 7 10 8 55 24
6 14 40 3 1 7 10 8 24 55
```

Then, during the next iteration of the inner loop, we see that the 40 is moved to the second highest position, and so on. In each iteration of the inner loop, we get at least one element in its correct position within the list.

6.3 SELECTION SORT

A **selection sort** is a sort that places an item in the correct location with each pass. Only necessary exchanges are made. For example, we could implement a selection sort that finds the largest item in the list, and swaps it into the last place of the list. Then, we find the second largest, and put it in the second to last position, and so on, until we have a sorted list. Likewise, you could do an opposite implementation where you find the smallest item and put it first, then next smallest in the second position, and so on.

6.3.1 AN IMPLEMENTATION OF SELECTION SORT

```
1   void SelectionSort(int a[], int size)
2   {
3        int minimum = 0;
4        int temp = 0;
5
6        for(int i = 0; i < size-1; i++)
7        {
8             minimum = i;  //assume this is index of minimum for now
9             for(int j = i+1; j < size; j++)
10            {
11                 if(a[j] < a[minimum])
12                 {
13                      minimum = j;
14                 }
15            }//end inner loop
16
17  // swap the next smallest item
18  // we've found into the right location
19            if(i != minimum)
20            {
21                 temp = a[i];
22                 a[i] = a[minimum];
23                 a[minimum] = temp;
24            }
25       }//end outer for
26  }
```

This particular implementation finds the next minimum item in the array at each pass through the array. The way in which this works is to store the *index* of the minimum item. At the beginning, on line 8, we assume that the element at *i* is the minimum element. Then, we move through every element after I through the end of the array, which is why we start at i + 1 on line 9 in the header of the inner for loop. If we find an element a[j] that is *less* than our current minimum element, we set the new minimum index to j, as seen on lines 11-14.

After each iteration of the inner for loop, we swap the next smallest item in sequence with the current position *i*. The test on line 19 is to ensure we aren't swapping a number with itself – this is the case when the element at *i* is in fact the minimum, so there is no need to swap.

At the end of this, we have a sorted list.

6.3.2   AN ENTIRE SOURCE FILE USING SELECTION SORT

```
1    #include <iostream>
2    using namespace std;
3
4    void SelectionSort(int arr[], int size);
5    void PrintArray(int arr[], int size);
6
7    int main()
8    {
9          const int ARR_SIZE = 10;
10         int arr[ARR_SIZE] = {55, 6, 14, 40, 3, 1, 7, 10, 8, 24};
11
12         cout<<"Before sort:"<<endl;
13         PrintArray(arr, ARR_SIZE);
14         cout<<endl<<endl;
15
16         SelectionSort(arr, ARR_SIZE);
17
18         cout<<"Sorted:"<<endl;
19         PrintArray(arr, ARR_SIZE);
20
21         return 0;
22   }
23
24   void SelectionSort(int a[], int size)
25   {
26         int minimum = 0;
27         int temp = 0;
28
29         for(int i = 0; i < size-1; i++)
30         {
31               minimum = i;   //assume this is index of minimum for now
32               for(int j = i+1; j < size; j++)
33               {
34                     if(a[j] < a[minimum])
35                     {
36                           minimum = j;
37                     }
38               }//end inner loop
```

```
39
40    //swap the next smallest item we've found into the right location
41                if(i != minimum)
42                {
43                        temp = a[i];
44                        a[i] = a[minimum];
45                        a[minimum] = temp;
46                }
47         }//end outer for
48    }
49
50    void PrintArray(int arr[], int size)
51    {
52         for(int i = 0; i < size; i++)
53         {
54                cout<<arr[i]<<endl;
55         }
56    }
```

The output is as follows:

```
Before sort:
55
6
14
40
3
1
7
10
8
24


Sorted:
1
3
6
7
8
10
14
24
40
55
```

```
Press any key to continue . . .
```

As expected, this output is the same as before. We just do this as a sanity check to ensure that our implementation appears to work.

6.3.3   A CLOSER LOOK AT THE ABOVE SORTING PROCESS

We start with the following unsorted list:

55   6   14   40   3   1   7   10   8   24

If we print out the list, after each loop through the list, we will get the following:

```
55 6 14 40 3 1 7 10 8 24
1 6 14 40 3 55 7 10 8 24
1 3 14 40 6 55 7 10 8 24
1 3 6 40 14 55 7 10 8 24
1 3 6 7 14 55 40 10 8 24
1 3 6 7 8 55 40 10 14 24
1 3 6 7 8 10 40 55 14 24
1 3 6 7 8 10 14 55 40 24
1 3 6 7 8 10 14 24 40 55
```

Although the resulting sorted list is the same, you can see quite clearly that the number of actual swaps being performed is far less than with our Bubble sort example. Note that with each line of the above output, the smallest element in the entire list is found (1) in the location in the array at 5 (the 6th position), and that the 1 and the 55 are swapped. Then, we move on to the *second* largest element. That element is found, namely the number 3, at the 5th position (index 4) and swapped with the second item. So, we swap the 3 and the 6. This continues, with the next smallest element being selected after each iteration.

6.4   INSERTION SORT

An **insertion sort** is a sort in which we insert items into an already sorted list. This is similar to how we inserted items into our sorted linked list implementation. We can think of our scheme as partitioning our array into two sets: a sorted set and an unsorted set. First, we start with one element. Obviously, if there's only one element in the set, it's sorted. Then, add the next element, making our sorted list one larger, and the unsorted list one smaller. You add it to the correct location within the sorted side of the array. Continue until the entire array is sorted.

6.4.1   AN IMPLEMENTATION OF INSERTION SORT

```
1    void InsertionSort(int a[], int size)
2    {
3          int temp = 0;
4          int j = 0;
5
6          for(int i = 1; i < size; i++)
7          {
8                j = i;
9                while(j > 0 && a[j-1] > a[j])
10               {
11                     temp = a[j];
12                     a[j] = a[j-1];
13                     a[j-1] = temp;
14                     j--;
15               }
16          }
17   }
```

In this implementation, we use the outer loop to start at the second index (1), initializing the counter for the inner `while` loop (`j`) to `i` on line 8. With this implementation, we look at the element below `j` as long as `j` is greater than 0 (in other words, at least 1.) We swap until the element is in its correct position.

Note that we move down toward 0 in the inner loop, so we essentially move the element at `a[j]` into its correct position. We continue (in the outer loop) until we have added all of the elements to our newly sorted list.

6.4.2 AN ENTIRE SOURCE FILE USING INSERTION SORT

```
1   #include <iostream>
2   using namespace std;
3
4   void InsertionSort(int arr[], int size);
5   void PrintArray(int arr[], int size);
6
7   int main()
8   {
9         const int ARR_SIZE = 10;
10        int arr[ARR_SIZE] = {55, 6, 14, 40, 3, 1, 7, 10, 8, 24};
11
12        cout<<"Before sort:"<<endl;
13        PrintArray(arr, ARR_SIZE);
14        cout<<endl<<endl;
15
16        InsertionSort(arr, ARR_SIZE);
17
18        cout<<"Sorted:"<<endl;
19        PrintArray(arr, ARR_SIZE);
20
21        return 0;
22   }
23
24   void InsertionSort(int a[], int size)
25   {
26        int temp = 0;
27        int j = 0;
28
29        for(int i = 1; i < size; i++)
30        {
31              j = i;
32              while(j > 0 && a[j-1] > a[j])
33              {
34                    temp = a[j];
35                    a[j] = a[j-1];
36                    a[j-1] = temp;
37                    j--;
38              }
39        }
40   }
41
42
43
44   void PrintArray(int arr[], int size)
45   {
```

```
46        for(int i = 0; i < size; i++)
47        {
48            cout<<arr[i]<<endl;
49        }
50  }
```

The output is as follows:

```
Before sort:
55
6
14
40
3
1
7
10
8
24


Sorted:
1
3
6
7
8
10
14
24
40
55
Press any key to continue . . .
```

6.4.3   A CLOSER LOOK AT THE ABOVE SORTING PROCESS

We start with the following unsorted list:

55   6   14   40   3   1   7   10   8   24

If we print out the list, after each iteration of the outer loop, we will get the following:

```
55  6  14  40  3  1  7  10  8  24
6  55  14  40  3  1  7  10  8  24
6  14  55  40  3  1  7  10  8  24
6  14  40  55  3  1  7  10  8  24
3  6  14  40  55  1  7  10  8  24
1  3  6  14  40  55  7  10  8  24
1  3  6  7  14  40  55  10  8  24
1  3  6  7  10  14  40  55  8  24
1  3  6  7  8  10  14  40  55  24
1  3  6  7  8  10  14  24  40  55
```

In the above, I have the original array listed at the top, and then, on the second line we add the second number (the 6) in a sorted fashion, then the 14 (which falls between the 6 and the 55) and so on. The bold represents our "current sorted partition" of the array, whereas the unsorted partition is not bolded.

APPENDIX A

A-1   EXCEPTION HANDLING

This is a brief review of the topic of **exception handling**, where we detect and correct errors, or at very least, *fail gracefully*. An **exception** is, like its name suggests, something that goes against expected or normal operating behavior. An example would be going out of bounds in an array. No one likes to see a big mean error message when your program crashes with a bunch of memory address information and scary numbers everywhere. It's much better if you handle your own exceptions rather than letting the operating system do it for you.

To handle exceptions, we use **try-catch** statements.

Exception handling mechanisms in C++ allow us to do three things:

- Detect an exception
    - This is done in the **try** block
- Tell the system that an exception occurred
    - This is done by a **throw** statement
    - Called **throwing an exception**
- Handle the exception
    - This is done in the **catch** block
    - Handling is what we do to respond to a thrown exception

A-1.1   REVISITING OUR STACK CLASS WITH EXCEPTION HANDLING

Previously, when we wrote our stack class, we printed out a statement to tell the user that the stack was full, or the stack was empty. We have many options to implement exception handling, including implementing a class that inherits from the `exception` class in the `exception` library. However, you can `throw` just about anything (even the kitchen sink if your plumbing skills are adequate!)

For our example, we'll keep things simple by basically declaring a class skeleton for our full and empty exceptions.

At the top of the Stack specification file, we can simply declare two classes, as follows:

```
1   class FullStackEx { };
2   class EmptyStackEx { };
3
4   class Node
5   {
6   public:
7           int mData;
8           Node* mNext;
9   };
10
11  class Stack
12  {
13  public:
14          Stack();
15          ~Stack();
16          bool isFull() const;
17          bool isEmpty() const;
18          void Push(int item);
19          int Pop();
20          int Top() const;
21          void MakeEmpty();
22          void PrintStack();
23  private:
24          Node* mTop;
25  };
```

Note that the only real changes we made were on lines 1 and 2 above. Note that since in this implementation, we are just going to be using the classes to identify the type of exception, we don't implement any member function or declare any data members. If you inherit from the exception class however, you should implement the what member function for example.

Now that we have our specification (.h) file updated, let's modify the implementation file slightly so that the Push and Pop functions will throw exceptions.

```
1    void Stack::Push(int item)
2    {
3            if(!isFull())
4            {
5                    Node* newNode = new Node();
6
7                    newNode->mData = item;
8                    newNode->mNext = mTop;
9                    mTop = newNode;
10           }
11           else
12           {
13                   throw FullStackEx();
14           }
15   }
16
17   int Stack::Pop()
18   {
19           int retVal = 0;
20
21           if(!isEmpty())
22           {
23                   Node* temp = mTop;
24
25                   mTop = mTop->mNext;
26                   retVal = temp->mData;
27                   delete temp;
28           }
29           else
30           {
31                   throw EmptyStackEx();
32           }
33
34           return retVal;
35   }
```

Pay special attention to lines 11-14, and also lines 29-32. We are simply throwing each of the appropriate exceptions depending on whether we have a full stack, or an empty stack.

So we have the "alert" being sent to the system with the throw statement. But what about the detection and the handling part of exception handling? That takes place in the main file, which has been modified thusly:

```
1    #include <iostream>
2    #include "Stack.h"
3    using namespace std;
4
5    int main()
6    {
```

```
7            Stack myStack;
8
9        try
10       {
11               myStack.Push(10);
12               myStack.Push(15);
13               myStack.Push(12);
14               myStack.Push(100);
15               myStack.Push(50);
16
17               myStack.PrintStack();
18               cout<<endl;
19
20               myStack.Pop();
21               myStack.Pop();
22
23               myStack.PrintStack();
24               cout<<endl;
25
26               myStack.Push(500);
27               myStack.Push(45);
28
29               while(!myStack.isEmpty())
30               {
31                       cout<<myStack.Pop()<<endl;
32               }
33
34               //pop on empty stack
35               myStack.Pop();
36       }
37       catch(FullStackEx ex)
38       {
39               cerr<<"You tried pushing onto a full stack"<<endl;
40       }
41       catch(EmptyStackEx ex)
42       {
43               cerr<<"You tried popping from an empty stack"<<endl;
44       }
45       return 0;
46  }
```

Firstly, we surround our **critical region**, that is, the portion of the code that might throw an exception, with a `try` block from lines 9 – 36. Then, on lines 37-40 we handle the exception if we try pushing onto a full stack. On lines 41-44, we handle the exception if we try popping from an empty stack. Note that the code that was executing would terminate from the point the exception was thrown in lines 9-36 and would immediately go to one of the catch blocks. In the above implementation, we write a statement on line 35 that will cause an exception.

The output proves this to us.

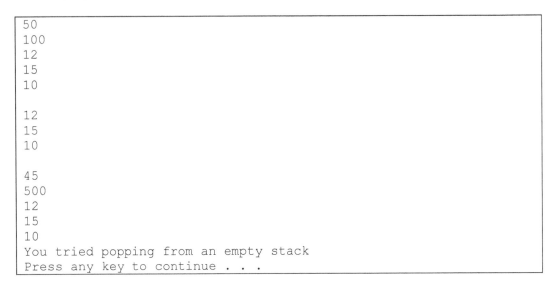

```
50
100
12
15
10

12
15
10

45
500
12
15
10
You tried popping from an empty stack
Press any key to continue . . .
```

Note specifically the statement at the end before the "Press any key to continue" statement. We can see clearly that an exception was caught.

As an exercise, update the code from the `UnorderedList`, `OrderedList`, and `Queue` to contain exception handling code.

INDEX OF TERMS

accessors, 10
ADT (abstract data type), 17
Big-Oh, 79
Bubble sort, 80
call stack, 52
complexity analysis, 79
complexity categories, 79
complexity classes, 79
composition, 18
critical region, 97
data members, 4
dynamic array, 16
exception, 25, 94
exception handling, 94
exchange sorts, 80
first in, first out (FIFO), 64
function call stack, 52
Getters, 10
heap, 14
implementation file, 4
insertion sort, 90
last in, first out (LIFO), 51
linked structure, 16

linked structures, 16
macros, 12
member functions, 4
mutators, 11
new keyword, 14
Node class, 17
nullptr, 17
Object-oriented programming (OOP), 4
private, 4
project, 5
protected, 4
queue, 64
scope resolution operator(: :), 13
selection sort, 85
Setters, 11
short circuiting, 30
solution, 5
specification file, 4
stack, 51
throw, 94
try-catch, 94
unordered list, 16